Dear ANORAK friends,

As you may have heard, we have been spending the last few months celebrating our tenth anniversary with a never-ending party. It is not over yet! We thought we'd extend the fun a bit more with a yummy theme: CAKES.

Since we are a team devoted to ensuring our readers get the best of the best, we spent a lot of time researching and testing this scrumptious subject matter. Tough job, I know.

Here's the result of a lifetime of 'research': a delicious edition exploring why CAKES are fun and where they come from. We have even attempted to produce a Top Ten guide – when really, we love them all!

One word of caution before you dive in: however tasty this issue might look, please do not attempt to bite into it. If you do, we cannot be held responsible for any funny tummies. Enjoy!

The Extraordinary Tale of the Dog who Turned Human (For One Day)

Florian had had enough of being JUST A DOG.
He felt trapped in the same routine day in, day out.

SLEEP. GO TO THE PARK. SLEEP.
EAT. SLEEP. BACK TO THE PARK. SLEEP.

WHERE HAD ALL THE FUN GONE?

"I am SO bored of this dull life,"
he confessed to his friend, Doris the Dachshund.
"You just need to wake up and see what a wonderful life us dogs have,"
she replied optimistically.
"I wish I was a human," he replied.
"O-ho. Careful what you wish for!" she warned him.

From that moment on, Florian woke up
every morning wishing he was a human.

He wished with all his might
that something, somehow,
would get him out of his
wretched dog state.

Nothing happened for a week... until one morning,
as he was stretching after a long night's sleep, Florian noticed something odd:
he had hands! *"By Anubis, my wish has been granted! Hooray!"*
Florian got up and wobbled around on his two newly-acquired feet.
"Wait till Doris sees me," he thought. As it turned out, Doris was not impressed.
At first she didn't recognise him in his human form, and then she disapproved.

"Doris! It is me, Florian!"
*"What? You look NOTHING
like the Florian I know!
You have no hair!"*
she answered, aghast.
*"I wished Doris, I wished so hard that
it happened! I am now a human."*
"That's too odd Florian. Goodbye."

Florian was a tad upset by his best friend's rejection: dog or human,
he was still the same inside. As he was brooding on a bench,
he was interrupted by a strange sight in front of him. A squirrel had approached
and was looking at him with begging eyes.

Florian couldn't resist. He had to run after him!
But his two legs were not as fast as his previous four.
He soon lost track of the squirrel. He even tried to smell
its track by bending down on all fours, but the trace was gone.

"It's slow being a human," thought Florian.
"Four legs are definitely better than two!"

Florian spotted two humans.
"I am the same as them now.
Time to make some new friends," he thought.
He leapt to his (two) feet and ran towards them.
He excitedly jumped on them, licked their faces
and even attempted to sniff their bottoms.

Alarmed by such overwhelming displays of affection,
the humans ran for their lives to the other side of the park.
Florian was puzzled.

"It's lonely being a human," noted Florian.
"What's wrong with a bit of friendliness?"

He became hungry and decided to stop at *Chez Chienne*, the town's café.
Upon entering, he was encouraged by how welcoming the humans were.
When he was a dog, he had often had to wait outside.
"Finally!" he thought. *"There are some benefits to this new appearance!"*
He sat at a table and was handed a menu, but he realised
that he hadn't learned how to read. He just pointed
at an item on the menu, and that seemed to do the trick.

The waiter arrived with a large plate of spaghetti.
"Yummy," thought Florian, *"wriggly worms."*
He lowered his head into it, opened his mouth wide
and gobbled up the whole lot.
"That was a small portion," he growled.
He looked around and was surprised to see that everyone
was staring at him with scrunched-up faces.
"It's no fun being a human," thought Florian.
"They have no idea how to enjoy food."

Florian walked through town, sniffing here, peeing there
and feeling more and more downcast.
He went home and sat in his garden, wondering what could make
his new life better. He had tried friends,
exercise and food, but none of these human activities had satisfied him.
"Only a true friend can help me now," Florian hoped.

He called for Doris by barking loudly.

She arrived and her first words were:
*"I cannot look you in the eyes Florian.
You are too odd-looking."*

*"Please Doris, forgive me.
Look at me and please help me.
Being a human is over-rated.
No-one wants to run with me
and I am not even enjoying the food!"*

*"I am not a magician, Florian, nor a fairy!
You need to do a reverse wish,
and you might return
as a dog in the morning."*

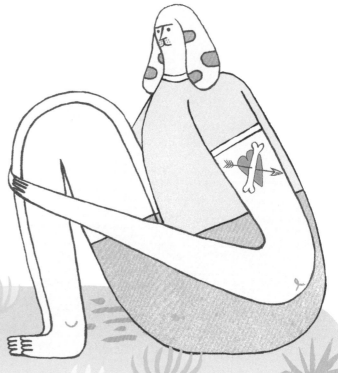

Florian spent the whole night in his kennel, wishing and wishing.
In the morning, he had returned to being a normal dog.

"Doris, will you be my friend now?" he asked his pal as they met again in the park.
"Yes Florian – provided you never wish to be something else ever again," she replied.
"Promise! Although, being a squirrel looks like so much fun…" he started.
Doris cut him short. *"NO Florian!"*

THE END... *(or maybe not.)*

PABLO the PASTRY CHEF

WORDS BY CATHY OLMEDILLAS   ILLUSTRATIONS BY VINNIE NEUBERG

Ever since he was a child, Pablo's dream was to be a pastry chef.
After school, he would run to his home and spend hours in his garden,
creating secret recipes for his friends.

He acquired many fans over the
years: Sarah the Snail loved
his Lettuce Layer Cake,
while Frida the Frog loved his
Worm Wedding Cake.

Around the age of 12, Pablo felt ready to share his talent with creatures other than the loyal friends he had made in his back yard.

He decided it was time to open his very own café. He went to the woods, picked up tons of branches and built a nice-looking hut, complete with a low table, two cushions for chairs and wild flowers for decoration.

He drew a sign and proudly perched it on top of the hut.

He prepared for his grand opening by spending hours inventing, cooking and testing recipes.

After a couple of weeks of intense research, he decided he was ready to open to the public.

His first guests would be his family and if they liked it, he would invite all his neighbourhood.

That Saturday, after lunch, he proudly announced that **PABLO'S PASTRY PARADISE** was open for business. He led his Mum, Dad and Dog the dog to his establishment and handed them the menu.

Mum and Dad looked at each other and both opted for the vegetarian menu.
Pablo couldn't convince them to try any of the meaty options.
Dog the dog enthusiastically pointed his nose at the Roasted Spiders Tart. "Good choice, Dog," shouted Pablo.

All of them enjoyed it thoroughly and congratulated the budding chef.

Spurred on by this first success, Pablo invited Paula and Peter,
two of his best friends, for a free tasting afternoon.

He was quite surprised to discover that they too only wanted to try
the vegetarian option. Pablo questioned them and Paula admitted that
Roasted Spiders or Caterpillars sounded just too strange – it was
something other animals might eat, but not humans.

His two friends offered their congratulations
on the Lavender Cupcakes and promised to come back.

Except they never did.
Pablo was puzzled and a tad disheartened.
He had no intention of becoming one of those boring chefs
who only use sugar, flour and chocolate.
As the days went past and customers were getting
rarer and rarer, he had to face the truth:
his food was too strange for human consumption.

One evening, Frida hopped by and noticed Pablo sitting in his café, looking gloomy. She asked why he wasn't cooking his usual delicious food. He explained that no-one seemed to enjoy it.

"Nonsense!" she croaked. She urged him to carry on as it was the most delicious food that all of her garden pals had ever eaten.

"Why not cater just for us since we love it so much?" she suggested.

The following afternoon, **PABLO'S PASTRY PARADISE** reopened for business. Frida had done an excellent job promothing this happy event and dozens of garden pals arrived to taste Pablo's new recipes. All had a very enjoyable tea of Slug Sweets, Crickets Cheesecake and Grubs Gateau. They all promised to come back. And they did, by the dozens. The day after, the month after, the year after.

Pablo never again had to worry about what humans thought of his culinary skills.

He went on to become the Greatest Chef the Garden had ever seen, and was even invited to make delicacies for other gardens in the Kingdom.

The Bugs Alphabet

Pictures by Jay Daniel Wright
Words by Cathy Olmedillas

A for Ant

B for Buzzing

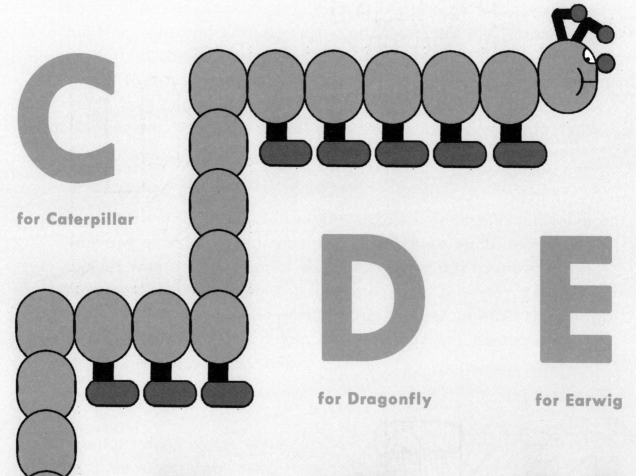

C for Caterpillar

D for Dragonfly

E for Earwig

F for Flying

G for Grasshopper

H for Honey

I
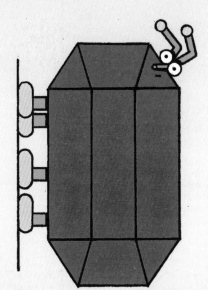

for Insect

J

for Jewel
Beetle

K

for Kissing Bug

L

for Ladybird

M

for Mosquito

N

for Nit

O

for Owlfly

P

for Praying Mantis

Q

for Queen Bee

R

for Roach

S

for Spider

T

for Termite

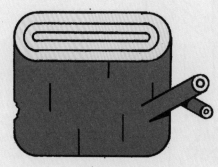

U

for Underwing

V

for Vespula

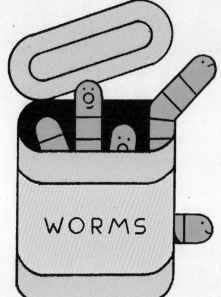

W

for Worm

X

for Xylodromus

Y

for Yellow Jacket

Z

for Zoraptera

THE SILLY TOUR OF LONDON

Written by Cathy Olmedillas

Illustrations by Andrea Chronopoulos

"Jump on board, dear friends, for a tour of London – a tour like no other.

Come with us to explore the weirdest, strangest

and most unbelievable tales London has to offer.

Please note that to enjoy this tour fully, you may want to leave

all rational thoughts behind and instead switch your imagination cells on."

"Here lived the most famous detective of all time. At this exact spot, on the 12th May 1906, he dropped his pipe. On that same day, the Prime Minister of Great Britain, when at the Houses of Parliament, dropped his pipe. There ensued a case of 'pipe dropping' like the country had never seen. This epidemic reached silly proportions throughout the day but, at exactly midnight, it stopped. Since that day, no other pipe incidents have ever been reported."

"As you may know, Martians once lived in London but they left around the 8th Century because they didn't like the food. A few months of daily cabbages, beans and raw fish proved too much for their intergalactic tastebuds.

They also intensely disliked children running around in the streets at all hours of the day. They demanded that all children go to bed at 8PM, on the dot. They turned that into law and it is still in place now."

"We are now approaching the most magnificent
of all the statues in London. This is Bhanu the Lion, who famously escaped
from London Zoo in 1866. He is believed to have roamed around the city,
frightening everyone on his way. Despite many efforts by the police
and the army to capture him, he remained at large for a few months.
Until, one day, the people of London woke up to find
Bhanu mysteriously frozen on this spot. He has not moved since."

ANORAK and the BIRTHDAY CAKE

It promised to be a fun day at Anorak Elementary. It was Julia's birthday and all were looking forward to tasting the cake Julia had made.

Words by Cathy Olmedillas
Illustrations by Jürg Lindenberger

A KID'S LIFE...

SPINACH AND BROCCOLI, BRUSSELS SPROUTS,
MEDICINE, HOMEWORK AND CHORES.
ARITHMETIC, SPELLING, A TEACHER WHO SHOUTS,
MY DRAWINGS ALL OVER THE FRIDGE'S DOORS.

GREAT AUNTS WHO RUMPLE MY HAIR,
COUSINS WHO COME TO STAY.
I KNOW I SHOULD MEET AUNTIE CLAIRE,
BUT I WOULD RATHER GO OUT TO PLAY.

GOING TO BED AT SEVEN
WHEN EVERYONE ELSE STAYS UP LATE.
I WOULD MUCH RATHER WAIT TILL ELEVEN
THOUGH I MIGHT BE SLEEPY BY EIGHT.

THINGS I MUST EAT, THINGS I MUST DO,
RULES ABOUT WHERE I CAN GO.
MANY DOORS THAT I MUSTN'T GO THROUGH,
TOO MANY FOLKS WHO SAY 'NO'.

WORDS BY ROY EDWARDS,
ILLUSTRATION BY ELEONORA AROSIO

YOGASAURUS

Yogasaurus wakes up in the morning saluting the sun.
He goes to bed at night saluting the sun.
He is a bendy dinosaur, very adept at lunges.
He is proud of his headstand, which he has practised hard
over a period of 82 years. One day he hopes to master
a handstand but he has so far found it quite difficult,
because he has unusually small hands.

WELCOME TO

MAGICALDACTYL

Magicaldactyl is famous the world over for his impressive
magic tricks. He plays in many valleys to an ever-growing audience
of adoring dinosaur fans. With his incredible strength
he can pulverise meteors of any size. His favourite trick
is Sawing a Diplo in Half, which he has perfectly mastered...
after a couple of decades of mixed results.

DINOSAURS LAND!!

DUMBOSAURUS REX

Dumbosaurus Rex is the King of all Dumbosauruses.
Even though his brain is as small as a pea – a prehistoric pea,
that is – he is much loved by all dinosaurs for his great
sense of humour. His giant head is firmly stuck in the clouds
and, for that reason, he always seems to be falling off
enormous craters, much to the delight of his dino-pals.

CHATTYODON

Chattyodon was born talkative. Since birth, words have been tumbling out of his mouth in a never-ending stream. Most of the dino-community enjoy his company – they find him generally quite entertaining – but others would prefer crossing oceans to crossing his path. Chattyodon is hugely popular at the regular sporting events where he is, without fail, the commentator of choice.

Words by Cathy Olmedillas, illustration by Jay Barnham.

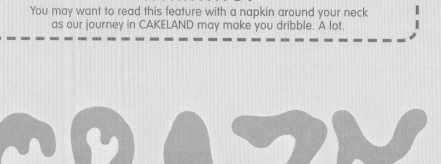

CRAZY FOR CAKES

Cakes are magical because with just a few basic
ingredients – flour, butter, sugar and eggs – we can create
so many different varieties. That's why we love
them dearly. Eating them is nice too, mind.
Here's a small essay in CAKE-OLOGY,
the science of loving cakes A LOT.

Cakes are amazing because they come in so many different shapes, sizes, tastes and colours: red velvet ones, blue ones, chocolatey ones, flat ones, tall ones, round ones, creamy ones and even beetroot ones!
In fact, they don't even have to have tons of sugar in them to taste good. Honey, fruits and even carrots are perfect cake sweeteners, so you don't always have to worry about rotten teeth or wobbly bellies.

According to Guinness World Records, the tallest cake ever made measured 33 metres high and 9 metres wide!
It was made by a cooking school in Indonesia and gobbled up in one mouthful by Gary the giant.*

If aliens came down to Earth and asked us how to bake a cake, the first thing we would teach them is… the Licking the Spoon rule.
This rule is essential in the making of a cake, whether you are 4 or 44 years old. Crucially, it means we don't have to wait a *reaallly looong* time for the cake to bake to enjoy it. Sometimes it is even better than the actual cake!

Of all the different types of cake, the most famous is the wedding cake. They are the oldest cakes ever made. Young Roman brides and grooms had wedding cakes made of wheat, which they would break on each other's heads!
In Medieval times, wedding cakes were stacked as high as possible and the bride and groom had to kiss over them, without making them fall down. Fast-forward to the 17th Century, and wedding cakes had a ring hidden inside them. The person to find it (or rather, to break their teeth on it) would be the next to marry... but not before they paid a visit to the dentist!

*that last fact is purely made up.

Christmas cakes come in all different shapes and sizes. And tastes. Our British one is super sticky, filled with strong alcohol and pesky raisins, and is frankly something that only adults seem to enjoy. A French Christmas cake looks like a wooden log and is made of chocolate. Definitely more palatable.

The King of cakes has to be this chap: Marie-Antoine Carême. Born in 17th-Century France, he went from being an abandoned child, living on the streets of Paris, to the most sought-after chef, loved by all Kings and nobles around Europe. Inspired by architecture, he was known for making fabulously decorated cakes in the shape of Roman villas and Egyptian pyramids. He is the inventor of many cakes we love to eat today, such as mille-feuilles, profiteroles and meringues. Merci Carême!

Anorak's Cake Hero is… Bruce Bogtrotter, the cake-loving schoolboy from Roald Dahl's *Matilda*. In this great book, young Bruce steals a slice of cake from his schoolmistress, Miss Trunchbull. He is, of course, caught. He is made to eat a giant chocolate cake, and by giant we mean humongously enormous – twice the size of Bruce, to be precise. Undeterred, he gobbles it all up, thus earning the respect of his schoolmates, but the wrath of the terrifying Miss Trunchbull.

Eat a cake and become a King or a Queen? Is that even possible? It is indeed. The three kings cake is one eaten every year on the 6th January in French and Spanish-speaking countries. A little figurine (a bean or a baby Jesus) is hidden inside it and if you happen to fall upon it, you are King or Queen for the day. You even get to wear a crown to prove it! Funnest cake ever.

Think birthday and you will more than likely think of cake. Depending on where you live in the world, a birthday cake will be round, featuring your favourite cartoon characters, or it will be made with fruits, chocolate or even vegetables! One of our favourite birthday cakes is the one our friends in Denmark make. It is made in the shape of… a person! It is left to the birthday boy or girl to decorate it with sweets, and also to cut it. Head or legs, anyone?!

The Black Forest gateau is one luscious cake, made with layers of chocolate sponge, cherries and cream. Over 100 years old, its name was inspired by a region in Germany called… you've guessed it… the Black Forest. Though it's made all over the world, it is in its native Germany that it is the most popular. It even has its own festival every year, where pastry chefs compete to make the best one.

Do you need to be hanging from the ceiling to eat an upside-down cake? No, not really. Because the upside-down cake does the upside-down bit for you! It is a nice spongy cake made with pineapples, cherries or apples. It is cooked with the fruits placed at the bottom of the dish. Once it is out of the oven, it is turned over so that the fruits are at the top. When you let it rest, the syrup of the fruits trickle down the sponge. Slurp!

Red velvet cakes may seem like they were invented last week, but it turns out that they are at least 60 years old. Their distinct red layers are achieved by using… beetroot! We think this cake deserves a new name: the Surprisingly-Delicious-Cake-Made-With-Beetroot.

Panettone is a delicious, fluffy, tall cake from Italy, mostly eaten around Christmas. It is filled with dried raisins, which are believed to bring good fortune. If you don't like raisins, don't worry – panettone comes in all sorts of flavours: plain, buttery, or with bits of lemon, orange or chocolate in it. It can be eaten on its own, toasted, or with a scoop of vanilla ice cream. All of the above, please!

Custard pie has been a popular dessert since the Middle Ages. South Africans have their own version, which they call a 'milk tart'. North Americans make theirs with pumpkins for Thanksgiving.
Our favourite type of custard pie is the one the Portuguese make, called 'natas'. In Circus Land, custard pies are used by clowns who love to throw them in each other's faces. We must admit we much prefer them in our tummies!

Queen Victoria loved this cake so much that it was named after her. The Victoria sponge – also called a Victoria sandwich – is a sponge cake layered with jam. We love it because it tastes good, but also because it is super easy to make. Find a recipe (your Gran will surely have one) and have a go: with minimum effort you are guaranteed to dazzle your family with your Victorian baking skills.

New cakes are invented every day. Take the cronut. It is a doughnut and a croissant all at once. This new cake, invented by an American chef a couple of years ago, is now eaten the world over. Would you ever imagine mixing chocolate spread and pasta? No? YES! Chocolate pasta does exist, and is best devoured with strawberries and cream. What delicious cake would you invent, we wonder? Get thinking and please send any experiments to us at the address shown at the back of the magazine!

TOP TEN BEST CAKES IN THE WORLD

We love about 20,000 different types of cakes. But for you, dear readers, we attempt the impossible task of listing our favourite ten.

PAVLOVA

This cake has a name that sounds like a Russian ballerina. That's because it was named after a famous Russian ballerina, called Anna Pavlova! The legend goes that she visited Australia or New Zealand (no-one can agree where, exactly) and inspired a chef to make a cake as light as she was on her feet. It is made by layering meringue and fruits, such as kiwis, strawberries, passion fruits, mangoes and any others that take your fancy!

SACHERTORTE

Just the name of this cake sends our taste buds into overdrive. This Austrian dessert is dense and delicious: it is made of layers of apricot jam, chocolate, and… more chocolate. Yumbo.

BATTENBERG CAKE

Originally from the UK, battenberg is made of delicate squares of pink and yellow sponge, topped with colourful icing. We love it because of the fun checked patterns you get when you cut into it. And it tastes nice too.

MAGDALENAS

These small and fluffy Spanish cakes, a bit like cupcakes, are best enjoyed at around 4 o'clock, after a hard day at school. They are also delicious dunked into a mug of hot chocolate. We love them at breakfast, too. OK, yes, at any time of the day, *gracias*!*

*that's Spanish for *"Give us more magdalenas, thanks!"*, or just Spanish for "Thanks".

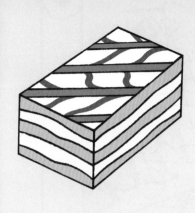

MILLE-FEUILLE

This French cake's name means "a thousand leaves". It's traditionally made of three layers of custard and puff pastry. (Not a thousand, then!) It is popular both sweet and savoury: Italians make a version of it that's layered with cheese and spinach. *Grazie mille!***

MOONCAKE

If the moon tasted like a mooncake, we would happily spend the rest of our lives up there munching on it. Originally from China, this delicious cake is mostly made of pastry, with a sweet red bean paste inside. It is sometimes made with crushed nuts, or even pork.

BROWNIE

A classic made mostly of butter and chocolate, it was first introduced at the end of the 19ᵗʰ Century by a chef in the USA, who was asked to make a cake that could be carried in a lunchbox.

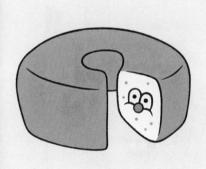

ORANGE CAKE

Oranges are delicious. Cake is delicious. So an orange cake is... doubly delicious! The Brazilians knew that when they invented the world-famous orange cake. Usually eaten at breakfast, this round cake with a hole in the middle is simply too yummy to eat only once a day.

MOCHI

Mochis are the "bounciest" of all cakes. They bounce under our teeth, a little bit like marshmallows. Made of rice paste and red bean paste, they come in all sorts of colours and flavours – and some are even filled with ice cream! Ice cream and cakes all in one? Yes please!

CHEESECAKE

It's the creamy texture of cheesecake that makes us love it so much. Believed to have been invented by the Ancient Greeks, we love how versatile it is. It works in many flavours, such as lemon, raspberry, passion fruit, and even our favourite: chocolate!

**That's Italian for "*Give us mille-feuilles*", or "Thank you very much".

SUBSCRIBE TO ANORAK

SUBSCRIBE TO
THE HAPPY MAG FOR KIDS!

Subscribing to Anorak means you get every SINGLE issue delivered to your door by a bunch of teddy bears on rollerskates.*

It also means you get FREE postage. AND you are guaranteed never to miss an issue.

To subscribe, get your Mum, Dad, Gran, Pops or any generous human being to visit

anorakmagazine.com/shop

Thank you!

*Please note that we can't always guarantee teddy bears as they often prefer to sleep all day.

Why do astronauts float in space?

When we think of astronauts floating in space, we often think of them
in space stations or on spacewalks orbiting the Earth.
Are you thinking that's because of gravity? Well, think again!
The reason they 'float' is because when they orbit the Earth, they are
in a state of 'freefall.' This is the same type of weightlessness
you experience when you jump off your bed and onto the floor.
Only, instead of hitting the ground in less
than two seconds, you never hit it - and you keep falling.
This is best demonstrated by the theory known as Newton's Cannon.
Imagine if you were to shoot a cannonball
from a very high mountain. If you shoot it with a little force,
it will travel a small distance and then fall to the ground.
If you shoot with more force, it will travel further.
If you shoot it with Hulk-like strength, it will travel far
and fall off the horizon, and continue falling forever.
Floating in space is like being a cannonball thrown with Hulk-like strength.

What is the sun made of?

More than 99% of the Sun is made up of Hydrogen
and Helium. Yes, the same Helium you might find in a floating balloon!
These are the smallest elements in the Periodic Table
and they make up most of our universe.
In a nutshell, the Sun is just a giant ball of gas - super-hot gas
that can reach up to 15 million degrees celsius!

What are comets and how useful are they to us?

Comets are icy balls of rock... or rocky balls of ice, depending on
who you ask! They are chunks left over from
when the "outer planets" - Jupiter, Saturn, Uranus
and Nepture - were formed. You can think of them as
the failed planets of the outer solar system, those that never
grew big enough to become planets in their own right.
Comets may have been important in the Earth's past.
Astronomers believe they are one of the ways that water
was brought to Earth in the first place: by comets crashing into it.

Words by Allison Hill (EU Universe Awareness)   Illustrations by Daniel Salmieri

BEAUTY IS FUN!

Sensitive souls, skip these pages now!
The beauty regimes of our ancestors could leave you feeling a little DIS.GUS.TED.
Or just very glad to be living in the 21st Century.

YUCKY BLONDE

Fashion-conscious Tudors loved blonde hair.
To get their locks whitened, they used... pee! Yes, pee
apparently has properties that can make one's hair blonde.
Surprisingly, they were not the only "shampee" lovers.
Vikings are believed to have used it
to dye their hair – and their beards!

HAIR TODAY, WIG TOMORROW

In 17th-Century France, there was a King named
Louis XIII who hated the fact that his hair was thinning
and he was becoming bald. So he invented the wig.
Here comes the strange bit: wigs were made
of goat, cow or horse hair, and attracted
many undesirable bugs, such as lice.
Bald, or itchy? What a choice!

PEARLY WHITES

If you were a rich Georgian and you had lost a tooth,
you could go to your surgeon and ask him to replace it with
someone else's tooth. Whose tooth, you may ask? Any
pauper who needed money could donate their teeth
for a few coins. The surgeon would simply sew it onto your
gums with a needle and a thin silver thread! Now if you'll
excuse us, we are going to go and faint now...

PEARLY BLACKS

The most revered of all Tudor royals, Elizabeth I, was a queen like no other. She was a great source of inspiration and she was incredibly popular: anything she did, others copied. Towards the end of her life she developed a sweet tooth, and sported very black teeth because she was eating too much sugar. So black teeth became the ultimate fashion accessory. Soon the court was filled with ladies with rotten-looking gnashers!

BAAAA-UTY TIPS

Interested in becoming as beautiful as a Roman? Easy! First take a sheep and chase it around a field. Once its wool is nice and sweaty, cut a bit off and rub it onto your face. That will, apparently, give your skin a healthy glow. Step two is all about the fabulous "Roman monobrow": simply burn a bottle cork and rub it across your face! Finally, if you have a few wrinkles, apply a little swan's fat onto them and they will just disappear. Voila! You are now officially as beautiful as a Roman…*

GLOWY HAIR

In the 1920s, ultra-bright glowing hair was all the rage. To achieve this Martian look, our ancestors covered their hair with a highly dangerous radioactive chemical called Radium! What did that achieve? A lot of sick people with glow-in-the-dark hair. In fact, they loved it so much that they also put it into toothpaste for extra glow-in-the-dark white teeth. The things one does for beauty!

*Actually, do not try this at home! You are beautiful as you are!

FOOD IS FUN!

Apples are just apples? Actually, there are over 2,000 varieties of them – and these are some of our favourites.

Red

The Red Apple earned a bad reputation in ancient tales, where it was mostly used by witches to poison people. But it is 10,000% safe, and possibly the sweetest apple ever known.

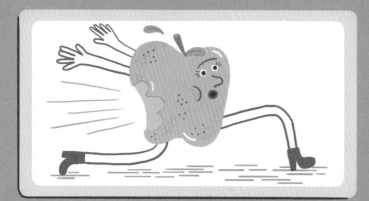

Pink Lady

The Pink Lady is not a lady, but instead a yummy type of apple with a pinkish skin.

Pink Pearl

The Pink Pearl is the most exquisite-looking apple, with its golden skin and bright pink flesh.

Bramley

Eat it raw only if you like super-sour food.
We prefer it cooked in crumbles, or baked in foil with a little butter and sugar.

Granny Smith

Named after an Australian Grandma who first grew it, the Granny Smith is best enjoyed in apple pies or covered in toffee.

Golden Delicious

The Queen of all apples, Golden Delicious are the most loved, eaten and grown the world over.

LAUGHING IS FUN!

What do you call a 100-year-old ant?

AN ANTIQUE!

What do you get when you cross a tiger and a snowman?

FROSTBITE!

There were four cats in a boat, then one jumped out. How many were left?

NONE, THEY WERE ALL COPYCATS!

What do footballers drink?

PENALTEA!

BOK! BOK!

Why did the chewing gum cross the road?

BECAUSE IT WAS STUCK TO THE CHICKEN!

On which day
do monsters
eat people?

CHEWSDAY!

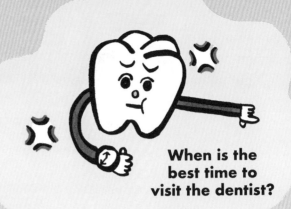

When is the
best time to
visit the dentist?

AT TOOTH-
HURTY!

Why was the broom late?

IT OVER SWEPT!

What's grey, stands
in a river when
it rains and doesn't
get wet?

AN ELEPHANT WITH
AN UMBRELLA!

What do you call a
stupid monster?

1 + 1 = 3

A DUMMY
MUMMY!

What does a mussel
do on its birthday?

IT SHELLEBRATES.

NATURE is FUN

ILLUSTRATION BY: Brad Woodward

RED ALERT

The red-lipped batfish is called "red-lipped" because - you've guessed it! - it has **red** lips! Our (unscientific) theory is that Mother Nature wanted to prettify a fish, but she applied too much lipstick and it got stuck like that. FOREVER. Joking apart, this fish is not only odd for its bright lips, but also because it can't swim. Instead it walks across the seabed using its four legs. Fishy, that!

FLAPPINGLY BEAUTIFUL

Try flapping your arms 50 times per second. NOPE. You can't. None of us can. The amazing hummingbird can. These delicate and beautiful birds can also fly on the spot! One thing they can't do is walk, as they have teeny tiny feet. They use so much energy flapping all day that they need to consume twice their body weight to keep going. We can't do that either. Although we have been known to try...

COW KILLER

We are not sure who is responsible for naming insects, but whoever came up with the idea of calling a panda ant a "panda ant" was a bit cuckoo. A panda ant is not an ant, it is a wasp - and it is not a panda, although it does look like one. It is a massive, furry type of wasp also known as a "Cow Killer", because its sting is so bad that it can exterminate something as big as a cow. Killer-Wasp-Pretending-To-Look-Like-A-Panda is what we would like to rename this ant. Buzzy thing.

PIGEON POWER

Poor pigeons. They don't get much love, do they?
We chase them, we eat them (some people do!), we curse them,
but isn't it time we showed them some respect? We should, as
they are, in fact, one of the most intelligent birds around.
For example, if you blindfold a pigeon and take it
to a random location, it will be able to find its way home every
time. Its clever brain is able to map any place. That's why,
way before the days of the internet or even the post office,
they were used to carry messages between people.
How impressive? VERY. Let's make a pigeon pinky promise
to never look down on them again.

PINK HOPPER

There is an insect on our beloved planet called a katydid.
Related to grasshoppers and crickets, it was given its name
because it sounds like the noise they make when they
communicate. The majority of these all-chirping and
hopping creatures are green, although some are pink, yellow
or even orange. The pink katydids are particularly lovely
because they look like toy crickets. They are super rare
and have a limited lifespan, as their beautiful colour
makes them a bit too easy for predators to spot. If you
ever see a pink one, consider yourself the luckiest
person alive: only 1 in 500 katydids are pink!

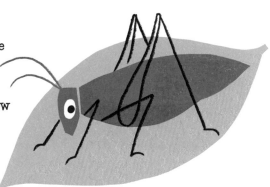

SMILEY STING

Have you ever seen a stingray's face? Doesn't it look like it is
forever smiling? But this is one smiley creature that's not to
be messed with. Directly related to sharks (gulp!), their sting
can be extremely lethal - because a stingray's tail is filled with
poison. You'd think that such a powerful tail would help them
to hunt their dinner, but they only ever use it in self-defence
against predators such as sharks and seals. As their eyes are
on top of their head, it is hard for stingrays to see anything
in front of them, so instead they locate yummy shrimps
using their keen sense of smell.

LET'S GO ON A BOATING ADVENTURE!

What will you bring along?

INSTRUCTIONS

- Make a copy of this page.
- Colour in your boat.
- Cut around it.
- Cut the plain lines.
- Fold the dotted lines on the inside and glue the white bits.

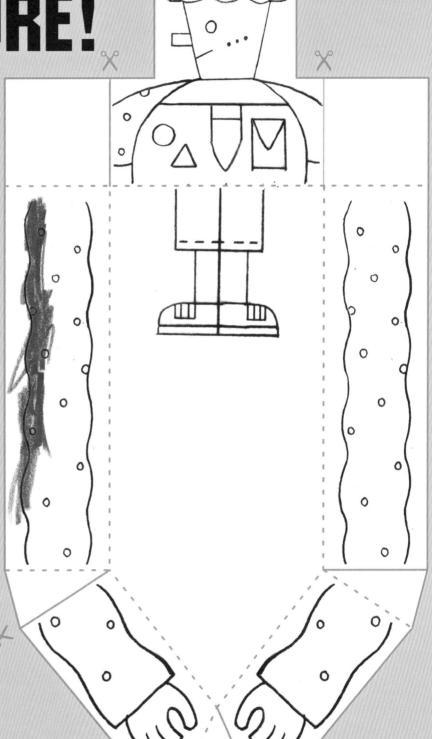

INSTRUCTIONS

Now fill your boat with the objects
you will need to take on your adventure.
Copy this page and cut out the items
you want to bring with you!

ILLUSTRATIONS BY JAIME JACOB

THE TALLEST CAKE IN THE WORLD!

HELP PETER THE PASTRY CHEF MAKE THE TALLEST CAKE IN THE WORLD BY DRAWING THE REST OF THE LAYERS

YUMMY WORDSEARCH

A	P	A	V	L	O	V	A	B	B
G	R	E	B	N	E	T	T	A	B
D	B	C	V	V	C	B	U	N	A
O	E	C	L	A	I	R	E	D	B
U	G	L	D	L	L	O	R	R	A
G	E	E	R	E	S	T	A	R	T
H	Q	S	E	K	A	C	N	A	P
C	U	P	C	A	K	E	D	U	P
E	K	A	C	T	I	U	R	F	R
G	M	O	O	N	C	A	K	E	F
V	E	L	V	E	T	E	K	A	B

BATTENBERG   CUPCAKE   MOONCAKE

SLICE   PANCAKE   PAVLOVA

DOUGH   ROLL   TART

BAKE   BABA   ECLAIR

BUN   ECCLES   VELVET

PUD   FRUITCAKE

COLOUR IN CAKE!

COLOUR IN THIS YUMMY CAKE USING THE CODE BELOW:

1 IS FOR BLUE   3 IS FOR YELLOW   5 IS FOR PURPLE

2 IS FOR RED   4 IS FOR ORANGE

PANCAKE

MAYHEM

LOUISE LOVES MAKING PANCAKES. A LOT.
CAN YOU COUNT HOW MANY SHE HAS MADE
AND DRAW SOME SILLY FACES ON THEM?

MY HAPPY CAKE

DRAW OR DESCRIBE YOUR FAVOURITE CAKE HERE

DRAW OR WRITE OUT ITS RECIPE HERE

NOW DON'T FORGET TO SHARE IT WITH US. TAKE A PHOTOGRAPH OF IT AND EMAIL IT TO US AT ANORAKMAGAZINE@GMAIL.COM. WE WILL PUBLISH THEM ONLINE. YUMMY YUM!!

ANORAK

THE HAPPY MAG FOR KIDS!

ANORAK MAGAZINE is the Happy Mag for Kids.
It is not currently available to buy in cake format but
we are in talks with a very famous pastry chef about that.

Boss & Tea Lady: Cathy Olmedillas
Cover & Feature Artist: Zhang Liang
Chief Designer: Mina Bach
Resident Poet: Roy Edwards
Editorial Assistant: Oscar Olmedillas Benady
Chief Wordsmiths: Tallulah Ellender, Danny Arter
Space Cadet: Allison Hill (EU Universe Awareness)
Super Talented Anorak Illustration Crew: Max Low, Nick Alston,
Jay Wright, Vinnie Neuberg, Andrea Chronopoulos, Jaime Jacob,
Daniel Salmieri, Eleonara Arosio, Chi He, Jay Barnham,
Lauren Humphrey, Jack Xander, Brad Woodward, Grace Danico

To keep in touch about Anorak news, please visit our website
www.anorakmagazine.com
For press queries, please email
Emma Lundie at pressanorak@gmail.com
For events queries, please email
Jenny Javens at events@anorakmagazine.com

If you would like to send Anorak a nice drawing or letter,
please use this address:
Unit L/M - Reliance Wharf
2-10 Hertford Road
London, N1 5EW

Or email it to anorakmagazine@gmail.com

To find out where Anorak is sold, please visit
www.anorakmagazine.com/stockists

To buy more fun Anorak stuff, please visit
www.anorakmagazine.com/shop

A BIG thank you to Reuben
(7 years old) for sending us
this lovely underwater drawing.

A BIG thank you to Edie (8 years old)
for drawing such an amazing
portrait of Anorak.
We all wish we had wings like that!